WOOD SPOKEN

WOOD SPOKEN

New and Selected Poems

Erling Friis-Baastad

Northbound Press

National Library of Canada Cataloguing in Publication Data

Friis-Baastad, Erling

    Wood spoken

    ISBN 1-896758-10-X

    1. Canadian literature (English) – Yukon Territory.
    2. Canada, Northern – Poetry.
    I. Title.

    PS8255.48F74 2004   C811'.54   C2004-980187-2

We gratefully acknowledge the support of the Canada Council for the Arts and the Arts Fund, Government of Yukon, for our publishing program.

Canada Council   Conseil des Arts
for the Arts   du Canada

Yukon
Tourism and Culture
Cultural Services Branch

Cover design: Arifin Graham, Alaris Design
Cover painting: *Trail*, 1996, Alice Park-Spurr
Author photograph: Copyright © Mike Thomas

Production: K-L Services, Whitehorse, Yukon

Printed and bound in Canada

Northbound Press
Lost Moose Publishing Ltd.
58 Kluane Crescent
Whitehorse, Yukon Y1A 3G7 Canada

Phone 867-668-5076
Fax 867-456-4355
lmoose@yknet.ca

For Patricia

A young man burns,
            of course,
again and again.
            Now that I'm old
one flame
            has reached the heart —
                  no longer obsessed
I am fully consumed.

Contents

Introduction

If death is followed by reincarnation and if I cannot come back as a human — say a trombone-playing search-and-rescue pilot — I'd choose to be an Arctic tern. The terns arrive in the Yukon each spring to breed and then, as fall approaches, head south again, flying across oceans, along the coasts of exotic countries I'll probably never visit and down to the sea bordering Antarctica, fishing as they go. They enjoy more continuous hours of daylight than any other creature on the planet, and travel further in search of it. Some cover as many as 35,000 kilometres annually.

One day in late July or early August each year as I walk along the Yukon River, I discover that the terns I've observed over the past couple of months — courting, guarding their nests, fishing, and feeding their young — have vanished. My love of *Sterna paradisaea* is tarnished by envy, for the birds go and I stay, winter after winter after winter.

However, brief periodic resentments of place are much like what can happen in any love affair. No relationship lasts for three decades, as mine has with the territory (with a couple of interruptions), without a longing for distance from the beloved other, a bit more room to experiment with a different identity. Many times I've thought that, if I could afford it, I'd settle permanently in Montreal or Madrid or Edinburgh. And so the years have passed, with me learning more about terns, about this territory, and — as will, hopefully, become obvious to the reader — about finding the right words for this place that has become home.

I stepped off the bus into Whitehorse on May 3, 1974. I was 23 and in those days relished long journeys by train and bus away from Toronto. So perhaps it wasn't weariness as much as fear of the new life ahead of me — or disenchantment with a rather homely little town whose snow had turned to mud — that caused me to write in my journal the next day: "Well, I've been in Whitehorse, Y.T., for almost exactly 24 hours.... The bus ride up the Alaska Highway was beautiful and rather fun: crazy good people and all, but I have a suspicion Whitehorse is a bit of a dead end."

The Yukon's best-known poet, Robert Service, arrived up here seven decades before me, shortly after the Klondike Gold Rush imploded. He wrote fantasies about the mayhem he'd missed in lines that sounded as if they'd been written by a frost-bitten Rudyard Kipling. One of Service's stanzas warns newcomers that we're bound to hate the Yukon "like hell for a season," but after we've hung on for a while, shed our naive cheechako ways, and become sourdoughs, we'll be as bad as the rest of the oldtimers, be in fact "worse than the worst." He meant, I suspect, that we'd patronize all those who are foolish enough to live Outside. And that happens, though it took me much more than a season to make peace with my isolation and distance from those nourishing centres of art, the big southern cities. Although I've never relished Service's sing-song whoppers, I've empathized with his life here. Many times I've become aware that my walks on the edge of town were following the trails down which he had fled his bank-teller's cage or his writing table. In truth, I probably had much more in common with his ghost than I did with anyone else up here back in the mid-seventies. At least he admitted to being a poet and took his inevitable lumps. I recall being introduced to a catskinner in Dawson City in 1975 who scolded, "Poetry is for women. Prose is for men!"

The earliest Yukon writer with whom I feel a strong affinity is geologist George Dawson, who explored a large swath of the territory nearly a decade before the stampeders arrived. He wrote *Report of an Exploration in the Yukon District, N.W.T. and Adjacent Northern Portion 1887.* His vision is elemental. Dawson didn't lose himself in tales of man-made chaos, but rather focused on the mysterious, almost frightening, order of details, such as rocks and fossils, that create the stage upon which our fleeting human dramas occur. I think Dawson would have approved of my later poems, especially lines like:

> Where sprigs of wild sage
> grasp at loess
> and a hot wind
> curries bone
> (from "Sedimentary")

But I was young when I first came to this place. I hadn't yet learned to look around me with the quiet patience and open-mindedness of Dawson. I couldn't have written those four lines then. What did preoccupy me was my own narrative: my adventures, my image, my laments. Models for such preoccupations were provided by poets associated with the San Francisco Renaissance, especially Lew Welch and Kenneth Rexroth, writers who frequently supported themselves by blue-collar work among the mountains of California and Washington. In fact,

3

I tended to view the Yukon in the seventies as my personal rural California of the fifties, and if I wanted to play at that, well, there was no one in the Yukon who cared enough to object. For me, the occasional jobs fighting forest fires, or hitchhiking toward the Arctic Circle on the unfinished Dempster Highway looking for work, were as much about travelling back in time as about the place I was actually in. As a result, the preconceptions that I imposed upon my poems overwhelmed the lessons the landscape might have taught me.

> For the past three days,
> we've been climbing
> up and down the burn
> on the side of our mountain
> toting pulaskies and shovels
> and "piss-cans" full of water
> until there is nothing left
> of the fire, not even
> a few smokes.
> ("The Last Night at Fire Camp #22")

That may be more about a young poet than an old landscape, but it's a memoir of an exciting week of discovery. And it was an essential step toward a poem that arrived more than a decade later, in which the narrator manages a few steps beyond the winter of 'self' and begins to recognize his small, vulnerable place in the ancient landscape:

> Some days, however,
> I discover myself to be
> exactly where I am,
> lost on a trail
> in the Yukon…
> ("Yukon Spring")

4   * * *

A brief explanation of my major editorial decisions is necessary. Over three decades, I've come to see the world and my art so differently that I could not revise old poems to fit new priorities without doing terrible damage. I am not the same long-haired, backpack-toting poet who stepped off the bus in the Yukon that distant May morning. But for all his limitations, my younger self was privileged to enjoy his own enthusiasms, discoveries and visions. That's why I've selected some of the older poems that now seem to me most significant. As a poem grows by a process of discovery, so does a body of work. No piece of a lifetime stands completely alone. I have made a minimum number of revisions to the older poems and have not attempted a rigorous consistency in punctuation. The newer poems are more sure in their music and more able to stand without the formality of punctuation, while the older ones would fall apart without the armature of convention.

A new and selected can be approached like a cutbank, in which layers of sediment tell a geological story that sheds light on how a landscape came to look the way it does and be settled the way it is. In fact, it occurs to me that the patterns and distances now flown by Arctic terns were established long ago, by the movements of continents and by ice ages. Had the Earth's plates shifted into different patterns, or the ice sheets endured longer or melted sooner, the tern flyways would be far different than those I envy today. Similarly, without youthful discoveries like those of "The Last Night at Fire Camp #22," visions like "Estrangement" would not have been possible.

Erling Friis-Baastad
Whitehorse

From THE ASH LAD (1988)

Bear Scare Stories

1

Fools and liars say bears won't hurt you
if you don't hurt them.

Who knows bear ethics
or the biographies
of all the bears they meet?

Somewhere up here, there's a mad mother
grizzly with your number on her.
She doesn't have anything against you
personally; it's just that her eyes are weak
and her memory strong.
She won't be able to tell you
from the idiots who tortured her
one summer.

A big sow was trapped in a culvert
by a work crew with a D-9. For nearly an hour,
they pounded on the culvert with hammers
and pipes. "Shoulda seen that dizzy bitch
stagger when we let her loose!"
the loud mouth
in the bar brags.

She's out there somewhere,
treasuring her headache,
biding her time.

2

There was a black bear,
small as a collie;
he lived last summer
at the Wiley camp.
The bear thought he was a raven,
hung around at the dump with a couple
and hopped just like them —
a big thing in a camp
where there's nothing to watch
but year-old wrestling movies.

Half the camp fed it on the sly
while the other half grumbled, "Had
my .308 up here,
I'd show that thing."

Rumour has it, someone showed him
when fall came, taught that little raven-bear
a lesson he'd never forget.

3

"There was a family a few years back,
shot some bear on the river bank
then sent the old lady down to skin it.
She was half done when the bear got up
and stumbled screaming away
without his pants."

The Last Night at Fire Camp #22

For the past three days
we've been climbing
up and down the burn
on the side of our mountain
toting pulaskies and shovels
and "piss-cans" full of water
until there was nothing left
of the fire, not even
a few smokes.
There'll be little to do
for the next 24 hours
but keep an eye open
for the chopper
that will take us home.
We look out over the delta
where the White River
dumps its volcanic ash
into the Yukon.
The sun set near midnight.
The sky was purple and gold,
royal colours,
and we feel like kings,
labourers lounging around,
swapping jokes,
digesting steaks,
drinking coffee,
taking it all in:
probably the first
and last men ever to sit
on the top
of this mountain.

Dawson City, Autumn

Once this morning
and once this afternoon
noisy flocks of geese passed over
going south.
Along the Pacific flyway
anxious hunters
are unracking their guns.
Here, on the edge of the Arctic,
it's over for another year.
The dancers and waitresses
from the gambling casino
have gone home to their universities.
The black-jack dealers
are off to Europe and Mexico.
The pit-boss is reunited with his wife in Reno.
Joe left with two women
and a fat wallet.
He mentioned Australia.
Those who did more drinking
than working on their claims
get up earlier than usual
and break into a sweat
over the ice on the puddles.
Those whose summer was all work
with no fishing
try to salvage it all
by bagging a moose.

The bars are almost empty.
You can hear winter's feuds
building in the low gossip
of the corners.
This will be my third winter in the Yukon.
I've gone back to walking in the hills alone.
I keep passing the old graveyards
just above town
thinking of all those sourdoughs
for whom Dawson City
was a one-way trip.

The Poet Divides His Time

I love too well
the place I've just come from
to ever be truly happy.
Twice this winter, I've picked up
and flown south. Twice
this winter, I've flown back again,
each time for good
and always.

Budweiser and shrimp.
        Heidelberg and moose.
Bourbon and lobster.
        Rye and grayling —

always the overpowering appetite
for the bounty of wherever I'm not.

This afternoon, I looked out
of the kitchen window
at Dawson City's snow-covered
Moosehide rock slide
and considered for a moment the myth
of the Indians who were trapped there
by an angry god, then
scolded myself
for being within sight of it again.

Wherever I go, I always come back here,
even from beautiful St. Augustine,
its pirate-haunted
narrow streets, pelicans,
margaritas and aggressive women
on the beach.

Friends in both towns shake their heads.
Bartenders greet me the same way,
"Hey, whaddya doin' here?
We thought you'd left!"

I make blushing, confused explanations.

From St. Augustine I return
through Toronto, Winnipeg and Whitehorse
to Dawson City and home,
with its spruce hills, two rivers
and the bar where I sit like some fixture
that's forever being sent out for repairs.

On Vilano Bridge

Porpoises are rolling in Matanzas Bay.
Along the bridge Sunday crowds
sullenly jostle for room
to fish. I am too poor
to presume to wave at the huge
blue sailboats passing by.
I wish I hadn't lost everything.
An intense young woman on a bicycle
issues me a significant "good morning."
I think she is testing to see
if I'm just another one —
too wrapped up in my own small thoughts.
"Howdy," I say, but she
is already a hundred yards away
and has me pegged.

Better Than Nothing

Early morning. Salt Spring Island.
I am sitting on the dock
staring into the channel, my brain
sodden, weighted down
and sinking past the sense
of your parting words.

An aged schooner
barely visible, anchored
in the mist
reminds me of Joseph Conrad
and of his men,
alone and hidden —
and then of you,
of course,
and the curiously erotic way
you have of keeping me
hungover and lonely
beside bodies of water
all over the continent.

From below, a jellyfish
arrests my thoughts.
I try to study
the perfect way
he executes his tasks,
pulsating, ingesting
and drifting.
No moods.
No traumas.
No brunettes.
I could sit here all day
with my indistinct awe. However,
I must rise and get back
to the full-time job
of living without you.

The Ash Lad

Mama and Papa and brothers,
Oscar and Peer,
have conned some befuddled sailor
out of a bottle of *Aquavit*.
They're stumbling
through the moonlight
while I curl by the hearth,
guarding our shack
and befriending
embers.

Outside, the wind screams...
or if it doesn't,
it should:
I am stirring coals
with Papa's favourite walking stick.

I'll be beaten, of course,
but no matter.
I feel lucky tonight
as if Gigantic Terror
were in the hen house
beheading the last
of Peer's chickens,
and Terror's wife
were snorting around the root cellar
coveting jewels of which
Mama had only dreamt.
In the morning, Oscar's heart
may be found frozen
to the top of our woodpile.

If my family only knew
what luxury scraps of bread
and dry cheese were to me
they'd have me survive
on the dried herring
that grow in the forest
and on acorns
that wash
onto shore
after storms at sea.

For the moment,
there is nothing to lose
and nothing is fear.
Someday, however,
I am fated to marry a king's daughter
and live in splendour
down in Christiania.
No one there will box my ears.

With my "X" on parchment
I will transform ragamuffin cousins
into fat civil servants
and live out my days
ringing up tea
for an endless queue
of pastors.

Meanwhile,
crouched on a cliff
above my childhood village,
an ugly troll
blinded with tears
will be trapped
by sunrise.

Local News

For the past week,
an exhausted young minister
has been locked away
in the back of the hospital
by his friend, the doctor.
All summer, young men of this town
have been taking their own lives
as if preparing for winter.
During each last breath,
the minister was catching his.

He barely had time to console
a wife, father, or mother
before being called off
by another disaster.
Every loud noise made him jump,
each splash in the river.
He lay awake nights
listening to hemp being coiled
on the far side of the world
in preparation
for his next failure.

Staid townsfolk complain
that their holy man consorts
with the loose and the addled.
The response seems so obvious
the doctor doesn't share it
with his sedated friend.
He whispers simply, "Hush for now.
Tomorrow, it may end."

Meanwhile, in some alley of that town,
a jug of cheap wine accompanies
a young man's brain into middle age.
His childhood friends
run in terror from his rage
so he wanders alone
and slack-jawed until dawn
when he'll steal a shotgun
and vanish into the poplars.

The minister calls out
from his sleep.

Spending Your Death in the Yukon

If the winter nights up here
are perfect for ghost watching
they're even more perfect
for being a ghost.

Imagine a soul — by day
it felt unclaimed and grey —
suddenly set aglow
by a bombardment of northern lights.

Then, picture that scene framed
by the leafless willows, encrusted
with hoarfrost.
They make good company,
                    like the ghosts of trees.

And the moon! The moon over all
this snow is so bright
even a shade would cast a shadow.

From CENDRARS' HAND (1990)

A Canticle of Ravens

All winter, ravens
have been hopping
from failed poem
to failed poem
as if wanting
to take over
and write
one of their own:

Ravens of creation
Ravens of death
Ravens of wisdom
Ravens of hilarity
Ravens of filth
Ravens perched upon mounds of frozen shit
on deserted streets
beneath a burning cold pink sky
after the best years of your life
have passed you by
and you are so lonely
pride fails you who
act overjoyed to see them.

                    Ravens
are the patrons
of our least comforting humanities.
They joke with wolves
but torment dogs.
Calm science cannot
contain them.
We can label them
Corvus corax
until we're blue, but

Corvus corax
when chanted in sorrow
until the spring thaw
becomes a curse
which turns back
to charm the chanter,
          some careless father:

Daddy has gone ahunting.

Daddy has gone ahunting
and a multitude of black-
feathered landlords
surrounds that unlit shack.
They squawk in tongues
to make impossible demands
upon his little daughter.

She wrings her ancient hands.
Daddy is never coming back.

Ice Fog

We are the people
in God's belly.
He exists in all directions,
infinite and grey.

There can be no world beyond
the crystals we drift among.
Only heretics hearken to sounds
other than the scream of boots
on frozen ground.

Once, we may have known words
for the many shades
of absence,
but through endless winter
have forgotten speech.

How foolish to imagine
lights in a sky
or the heat of lives
beyond the reach
of our numb hands.

Stranded

Memory causes the compass of the heart
to spin in all creatures
who chose to forsake water
for dry land.

Remind me again: a creek
leads to a river. A river
leads to the sea. I was calm
once beside the sea.

Today, past and present met
upon the ice of the Yukon River.
The February sun nearly blinded me.

That same sun once lured us up
and called us out — slow, awkward,
laughable miracles, dazzled by flowers.

Yukon Spring

Now that the snow has been beaten
back into small dour patches
between the black spruce,
I cannot sit still.
Each morning finds me
out hiking beneath
the new sun,
striding purposefully
as if I had somewhere
to go.

There seems to be a small
inarticulate religious fanatic
inside me. I must bear him
with me whenever I go
along the river and up
into the hills.
He makes me hum
some freighted tune
and I feel like an anonymous
composer of hymns
might have felt
long ago
in some Old World forest
with the latest plague
at his heels.

Some days, however,
I discover myself to be
exactly where I am,
lost on a trail
in the Yukon
but shorter

and darker
and stronger,
and carrying a burden
of still-warm flesh
across my shoulders
while making soft sounds
deep in my throat
of thanksgiving
and praise
and hunger
as night
races me home.

Cendrars' Hand

Blaise Cendrars' hand is high in the east tonight
Blaise Cendrars' right hand
severed by a bombshell in 1915
beckons outside my window

Cendrars' hand pounds on my window
                demanding in

                to grab me
                to shake me
                to drag me out
                by the scruff of the neck
                and give me a hefty shove

Cendrars' right hand
                makes a fist
Enough
        of this longing and lassitude
Enough
        of catatonia, of regret
        and of lying abed all day
        picking at memories!

Cendrars' hand points the way —
                                        South
this time
        Cendrars' hand aims its thumb
        at the road, "This
        is how it's done, kid!"

Cendrars' hand races across my typewriter's keys
Cendrars' hand holds a wild card
Cendrars' hand tosses a fistful of coins at the sky

I'm out
I'm running

        From the sidelines
     Cendrars' hand flashes signals
       all winning coaches know

      DON'T LOOK BACK

                   GO GO GO

IT'S A BREAKAWAY
under the dome
of Cendrars' hand
which is also skilled
at casting the shadows
of tropical dancers
on a screen of snow

From THE LAWS OF GRAVITY (1993)

For the Record

Paul Antschel
shall have no
name in the
Street of Exile

Paul Ancel
shall be driven
from darkness
into light

Paul Celan
shall leap out
of this world
at the end

of taking on
names: anonymous
word angel

Here, Now

Of course, you believe I am over-reacting
again, that what I heard was only a moth
colliding with the sea, a fish beating
against the sky, night getting into the garden

again. I tell you, what I saw was a girl
dragging a thin finger across wet paint,
erasing a nipple, smudging the sun, blurring
that scarlet line, the horizon

which once could prevent white earth
from falling into the white sky.
Have you never met a child
given to fevers contracted from books?

I read where it says,
    winter is past
I read where it says,
    the rain is over, is gone.
I read where
    flowers appear on Earth.

Now, you read where it says,
the voice of the flower says, cry

This Old Man

For your fingers, old man
a wall of shale and for your eyes
an ochre pot and for your heart
a stick

and for this small round stone
the gift of an old man's thumb

for the rest of us, astonishment,
terrible crystal,
adamant harder than flint

Writing the Novel
for Eve

I must leave your grandmother
in Russia, alone in the snow
with the wolves.
I'm sorry.

I am not the one
to take her hand and lead her on
to England, to South Africa,
to Canada, finally.

Finally, only you can do that.
However, if I don't look back
directly, but only glance
back from the corner of my eye

I can glimpse the path
the two of you must take. And
on this quiet evening I can hear
a few faint bars

from some old song
the two of you must sing
to keep your spirits up
on the long journey.

I can't quite make out the words,
but you will.

From THE EXILE HOUSE (2001)

Portraits of a Lady

Our lady was forbidding, her babe,
grim. Even their clothes hung
rigid and absolute until Cimabue
and Giotto allowed air in. Then,

robes billowed to fall in gentle
waves. Campin invited us to hold
the child — as if it were our own —
and we grew nearly filial with

the mom. But the boy became a man
and died and she, after a proper
interval, danced off to vanish
in the wild. Boucher thought

he spied her there, bathing
with a friend. Later, Renoir may
have glimpsed her, naked at a bath.
Manet claimed to have found her

naked too, dining in some park
with two clothed men. This proved
a hoax. Pollock splashed through chaos
on his hopeless quest. Rothko sought

her. He disappeared and left us staring
at an empty field. We're abandoned
to our loss, victims who celebrate
an orphanhood. We do have that,

at least: a small meal, if not a feast,
a final bit of nourishment before
we stagger home (gullible, slack-
jawed, almost dumb) to beg the absolute
        to take us in.

Filialis

Father, I tried
to protect you from me,
read late
into the Book of Orphans.

I studied a child
who went west.
He entertained his captors
by drawing horses

on old newsprint
with charred sticks.
I fled west, then north
and north again

until I could lie down
drunk on snow. It was
February, midnight,
fifty below

when I dared sleep
to come at me. But
some voice with no body
woke me, ushered me home.

Body with no voice,
be patient with my life
of promises. Accept
this incomplete angel

your foolish son
carved in snow.

Heritage

My father's name was Paul.
I don't give a damn
what anyone claims,
his name was Paul.

All those years,
while that other man
raised me, talking
of jackets and shoes

Paul hid in the forest
and gathered sticks.
No one knows if he
was building me a hut

or gathering fuel
for my fire.
He meant well,
as I do now,

dry and warm,
stacking bones
and moss
for my daughter.

The Strait
i.m. Raymond Carver

I walk beside the grey strait
and study on the far shore,
Port Angeles, USA, where you
once walked and peered out
under the risen mist
at my beach in Canada.
One of these days
I will cross this tossed
water in my own boat,
visit your old house
with all my friends.
It can be a small boat.
I haven't been sober long
and have saved few friends
from my drunken storms,
just Dave and Greg.
Though I have some new friends:
Pat, Eve, Rhonda, John and Joan.
I love them as I love this strait
in a wind which sets all
the exotic ducks to rafting
beyond the breakers —
scoter, pintail, goldeneye —
yet launches the winter gulls.
They remind me of poems by
Wallace Stevens and Hart Crane.
But that's as far as I'll dare
love today. I won't be taking it
further, to some bar, won't
be dragging my love out,
swallow by drop, to the dregs.
Tomorrow, I'll set off from here
again, beside the strait, early
before the crowds,

with the gulls and poets
stride part-way
to wherever their metaphor
would take me.

Badlands Jesus

There was this big sad man.
He sat down beside me
in a train in Montana
late one November.

The month was grey and flat
and the land was. You couldn't tell
where the land gave off and the sky
began. It got so bad there
with the big sad man I couldn't tell
where his life gave off
and mine began.

He was that hurt.
You know the kind:
they have lost most everything
but their thick spiral-bound notebooks
filled with their jottings on Jesus.

All this after "the wife" left, of course
taking the kids, and for good, of course.

"On this page we find Jesus and my great hurt…
Over here we have Jesus and the remnants
of my happiness…

Jesus holds many surprises.
Jesus appears in myriad guises."

Jesus once appeared to the big sad man in a dream
but the sad man recognized Him not,
thought he was seeing a dead shaman
who beckoned him down
into the arroyo where
the rattlers hole up come winter.

He was commanded to cut in
on the secret dance
of old bones
and woke up terrified —
didn't know where his arroyo quit
and that bed began. This
somehow saved him
and he tried to save me

as I read the notebooks
as I tried to comfort him
as I missed the scenery
missed the deer and coyote

as my sobriety
steadily failed

Like Love

My friend is not here,
the one who carries silver logs
for the fence, who
whistles the horses in
and whistles the horses
out, who knows all about
soft laughter and how
it must finally attend
all my missed marks.

She says, "Rest on this fence
beside the river and I will
describe your foolish talk
as something precious,
as something fine, like
an egg-shaped theory
about to evolve." Not once
have her numbers repeated
and we are further than
I have ever been to the right
of the decimal point
with no sign of rounding off.

How many people
have I met
who have the power
to forgive someone
like me? Only one,
my friend who is not here,
who sets the heavy logs
for the fence perfectly parallel
to the coulee
where I hide.
She uses no tools, just
her bare hands,
and adjusts us
by ear.

The Death of Saint-Denys Garneau

The heart fires off a line
                    that won't scan, then, ellipsis

The brain slowly quits its attempt
                    to count the cadence of silence

There is only one river, a grey page of evening
                    punctuated by tiny fish

He spins, seeking the path with no ends
                    then drifts off into a forest

as if Orpheus, by giving up his impossible art,
                    could be free

Sedimentary

this old hand falls
short of the memory rock

short of the sharps
short of the flats

settles finally, more loved
less perfected

where sprigs of wild sage
grasp at loess
and a hot wind
curries bone

The first angels to arrive in the interior

The first angels to arrive in the interior
were blown here from the coast
like exhausted gulls by a gale.

Dirty and lost, they recalled
only that they had hoped
to test man and tax him

— as they'd been invited to do
for those most mistaken
folk of the plains.

So this is how insomnia arrived
in the mountains. This is why,
during those back-country

summer nights, we stand up
one by one to wander the forest
where we collect our bouquets

of weeds and twigs and thorns.
And this is why, come dawn,
we are always so desperate

to drink any brew
that might dilute
a taste of salt in the wind.

The gods are changing face

The gods are changing face
again: He gods, She gods,
Goat gods, all the vast hierarchy
including the One and Only.

Sloughed off, a huge dry grin
drops. The down-rush of wind
staggers all before it. Women
stagger cursing into men.

Blacks cast charred fur
against the gale. Whites stumble
after burnt feathers. Day bursts.
An old forgotten night comes on.

Gibbering, we scurry back
onto familiar branches
while down below
lead-faced messengers

and spies with granite wings
form up awkward squadrons
        by the light
        of burning books.

Metaphysical Geographies

contemplatio in caligine divina

1.

Anything can be sung

fused, lobbed

the chorus can echo any blast
and sway

robes billowing
in each aftershock

2.

We once sucked sweet oil
from flinty rock, honey
from stone

We wander now, eyes
cast down
mewling for a second gift
of carbon

3.

Beware this frontier
its harsh face
broken
into promise
the lichen-splashed
rock glacier

but briefly
reposed

4.

Trumpeted

breathless

over the lip

into some valley of vision

each of us

flung

onto a cold canvas air

5.

"Ye shall speak into air"

finger
breaks in upon finger
that failing grip
dear old gesture
orphaned

6.

When the hymn forgets
its words

God listens

His variables
gone forth
multiplied

coda

When only the ineffable remains
you abandon your witless
vocables, leap
free from all kneeling
so quickly
a black beam
shatters

behind the eyes

Now,
you must feel your way
along the cold
wall

Fingers trace this journey
in a frost that cracks rock, ends
meaning, pre-
maturely.

The punch line falls away
drags you
in after it
writing

The climbing child staggers

The climbing child staggers,
stops, baffled. Who
has recalled the warm light

that had just been his —
reflected from the face
of this sandstone hill?

And who, suddenly,
has intercepted
a scent of sage

from the single triumphant sprig
that may yet cling
to memory-blasted rock?

Old Song

Everyone can love a dry
cold, a dry heat, a dry
eye in the house

it's such easy fortitude
such easy go easy
go

meanwhile, the quaking aspen
are quaking again
and it's only September

all of us chilled
all of us
all the way home

Boreal Summer

I wish to register my concern,
my distress, with this
annual suppression of darkness,
this revocation

of our right to stars. How
are we to locate ourselves
if we look up, only to discover
a few blood-stained clouds

in our sky? What's a little blood
to hydrogen? Each year,
we are misplaced. Believe me,
all that terrified tramps have cried

while stumbling in their circles
is true. By August, I am spinning
alone in the forest, trying
to summon faith, whistling

my tired air: *a sense of place*, just
another aging professional
at the peak of his career,
his season, his one day to mate.

Quiet

A recent study has revealed
elderly men are dying alone
in shacks in the forest.

They have sickened and slipped
through cracks in quartz
and timber, down

through woodsmoke and frost,
deep into the domain
of ancient wool.

They arrived here early
in the century, strong and thirsty:
They packed in accordions,

harmonicas, guitars...
then quickly became geniuses
of kerosene, cordwood and coal.

They are said to have sung
that last generation of wolves
to its rest.

Glacial Lake Whitehorse

At last, reprieved
by melting ice
an ancient lake fled
down our valley to the sea
              and never returned.

Without fish, sterile,
all its water ever knew
was wind.

Tonight, a dry wind
cries out for waves again.

The Exile House

This morning, lost again
I passed an old house
on a strange street
on my way home from the sea.
I suddenly craved to sit down
on its porch and wait
for someone to come to the door.
It was as if I'd lived there before
                and been happy.

Perhaps I waited too long
to tell someone about the old house
I wish I'd been raised in.
It was a huge dark thing
with many rooms
and a bright-red porch
beneath a sky so grey, the clouds
could have blown in from 1952.

If I'd sat on that porch and waited
I could have had a day like no other.
A stranger might have soothed me or panicked,
neighbours phoned the police.

I would have told them
that this was a house like the house
I should have grown up in, that
it was a huge dark thing
with many rooms. The neighbours
had feared the very idea of it, feared me
and barred me from school.

My only friends
were the ancient revolutionaries
who hid in the rooms.

They called me Little Shadow
and told me stories in their many
old tongues. They are dead now
and I've read too many books.

The Poet Attempts a Novel

My hero always fails me.
In Chapter One I give him everything:
height, youth, train fare,
a healthy moustache.
I encourage him to share
my family, my first wife,
the books I've read. All I ask
is that he be a man, push on
and meet his fate. But he
demands a rest at the first bend
we come to and slumps there
as if brooding on the injustice
of it all: the noisy typewriter,
the stubby pencil.
I do my best, change
his name from Darryl to Erik,
Erik to Darryl. The pages pile up
but he never smiles and rarely
speaks. Other characters
wander by, take one look
and disappear. Alone
he leans against my second chapter
thinking only of himself,
his words, his crazy music.

NEW POEMS

Wood Spoken

We are learning to bend close,
reach down to these —
logs, sticks, even boards

(though others have had their way
with them) recall home
and greener days

We are being called upon
to condense, to dip twigs
in primary colours

trace one bright line
across each life
or carve two letters
into the weathered wall
of some abandoned hut

Our initials will serve
There are already too many words

Prose

All the fevers have broken

The sun climbs willow, then spruce
Mist blows off

Swans head north or south

Earth meets sky
just down the street
and right on schedule

Nothing there is
must be said

though the voice is strong
and I am its eager
echo

Landscape

Everyone has vanished
from the recent poems
Every somewhat
human shape has fled

Sheets of slate lie naked
where wind has torn
familiar earth away
Sheets of silver bark lie

beneath the ruined trees
Stone and wood: perfect
open faces upon which
to carve new words

when time again
has need of them

The Window

The window: a poet's
most essential tool

Before it, he transcribes
a universe three feet
by two, rich literatures
of fog or frost,
rain's cutting edge

The skill is in knowing
on which side of the glass
the small moth dries
her invisible wings

on which face of the pane
the gnat sets out
on its fatal journey

And never press
your face to the glass
or the poem
will blur into prose

Towards Evening

As words fail, I learn

        Shameless I arrive

to rename the warm objects

        at your words, gasping

in your welcoming hut

        through your mouth

One is wrist

        You are that first wave

which turns

        and the last

to reveal a cupped palm

        to break over my face

from which my wavering double

        My hand clutches up

pours himself

        into your book

        while attempting to navigate

        through wine and wood and stone

Ghost Town

Winter widens gaps
in the log walls
of ancient cabins

then stars slip in
seeking their own
lost warmth

beams that fled
back when they
were blue, young

flames that found
once, a welcome
among us

Angelic

I've become strange again
but the city opened her heart,
set me beside the river

From the far bank
a willow answered
and a doe stepped into the current

If I don't look down
these wings might hold

The River

The river
this late in September
is the most lonely walk in town

The terns are long gone
the swallows, the gulls…

The last poplar leaves are departing

After a wet summer
high water wanders
among nearby willow
and wild rose
in search of loose twigs
and branches

anything
to ease its grey and
freezing back

Shy One

Who walks
a path by the river
each morning
so early?

Who casts her eyes
into the mist
above the currents
if anyone passes
but is easy among the terns
and gulls,
      if not always the eagle?

And she is at odds
with the magpies
and ravens, though
only the birds
themselves
know, they
are so like
her neighbours who,
as the sun burns off
the sheltering mist,
keep coming on
brazenly
down the centre of her trail
to greet her
in grievous error

Blockade

I never intended to live
so far from the sea
The boy I was
could not have fathomed
life on a mere river,
could not have fathomed
mere life

It is as if
the tide has gone out
                    and out

leaving dry flats
and fears and duties
while overhead
the same stars pass
again and again —
a flotilla that flies
the enemy's standard

After Guillevic

River, you are so
vulnerable where
you widen and slow

when you attempt
to be more
than moving water

Tell me
as I hesitate
here

while you
indulge yourself
in a marsh

will either of us
ever find ourselves
at the sea?

Estrangement

For thirty years
the small house
has dreamed she is a tree
fallen into the river,
giving birth to eddies
and hiding strong trout
in her shadow

and spring
after spring
the hill on which she sits
gives way
just a little
as the river nudges closer

A small dark figure
also lives there
on the edge
and each summer
he attacks the river
with a shovel and rocks

but his house
already shudders
in the rain

Atlin Lake

All night, the black lake
frets against basalt

fails to rid itself
of last year's drowned

In a cabin (only tethered
to dark by frailest chance)

again and again
an old man

is dislodged
from someone else's sleep

Fortune

No one knows
why rapids
suddenly decide

to forgive, or
a crevasse does
or a cliff

Here a mountain
chooses not
to topple upon us

There a river
confines its rage
between two banks

and we return home
convinced that our lives
are a matter of light

that one more day
has been handed down to us
through our eyes

Wind Instrument

You breathe this world
deep into yourself
then plunge
into the next

With each dive
you remain down longer

With each dive
you leave more of yourself below

Death Wish

Long ago, someone
cast off fur

leapt
into the river

She will drag you
onto her shore

tether you
to her forest

with stout babiche

Each new word
is a swimmer's stroke

Indigenous

Always, a lone audience
fenced off by pencils and pens

Bound by synthetic fibres
I have watched your ancestors

weave their dance
through wood and stone

But that was before
I discovered my name

carved into the rock wall
of a North Sea tomb

before I brushed
with my own eager hand

eastern fur, eastern iron
eastern ice, before

I heard salt-laden wind
polish my silver ring

What Then

What we call the next life
is not life

would be diminished by a word
if it could be diminished

hence my haste
my rude urgency

Only rhythm survives there
and tone, perhaps

All else is folded
upon itself

and into that
for which

we'll never
have the word

Evangelists

Perhaps they are
the itinerant monks
of a new dark,
these two at my door
in their black suits
on a grey day,
briefcases filled with fire.

Perhaps
the small burn of doubt
that lingers
after I order them away
is fuelled by a sliver
of charred oak,
a crumb of coarse bread,
wolf hair and other
wild rumours
from an age
of black horses.

My visitors
will return
when I forget
how to read and write.

A Forest Grave

A suicide
is buried here,
bones aligned
to the passing
of our nearest star

Set into a ring of river stones,
attended by soapberry
and wild rose —
he is shriven
by a raven's cry

Sepia

At night, to the north and south
the snow on our valley walls
reflects as sepia
the lights of town.

To climb there
then is to intrude
on an old photograph
like the ones that sometimes slip
from the pages
of neglected library books,
classics like our grandparents read,
perhaps aloud.

So much history
hadn't happened to them yet
but what had happened
was more clearly recalled:
lost ships and horses,
dead nephews and
the outrage of stride piano.

Meanwhile, aged labour activists
and young anarchists
still struggled toward better days
while wolf packs
left tracks
on the outskirts
of our largest cities.

Collaboration

At the far end of the grey lake
beneath damp mountains
a worked chert flake shines
from its cobbled bed
At last, the black blade
has carved its portal
through compacted centuries
Here, two makers meet
touch fingers chilled
from working the valley's
perpetual mist —
Pass it on

The Ring of Brodgar

Who raised these huge stones?

Astrophysicists in skins and furs.

Orkney's ancient Arecibo,
its Neolithic Jodrell Bank

now reveals

stars to lichen
lichen to stars

Warming I

What will become of our music
without black spruce?
What will become
of the clean tone we made
with a gentle tap
on a shard of ice?
Winter was beguiled.
A wind tamed.
Nothing is left to us
but Bible stories,
burnt parables,
sand

Warming II

Each of us once owned
a small portion of winter.
It became our legend,
not just some numb

pain at the furthest reaches
of our mortal portion,
but a nourishing goad
that called forth

the best in us. That
was then. Now, we marvel
at winter's broken back,
its feeble gesture

against the small, alien
passerines that stain
its white with tropic hues
and mock our fortitude.

Relevance

i.m. Peter Huchel

Now it begins, the gift
poets believed they'd relish,
announced at night
by hungry dogs
down unlit streets.

Now it ends, the old debate
on origins for lyric verse.
No instruments. Voice frozen.
The soloist suspended
in a web of state.

Has there not been

Has there not been
just one god overlooked
a small one, there
from the beginning

but lost in the shadow
of all those others, an innocent
who doesn't even know
the meaning of *damn*

— with no appetite
for sacrifice, who would
turn up sublime nostrils
at bull's blood, lamb's blood

and human blood, certainly
who couldn't care
if it's a he or a she, just this
That now drifting between stars

as among poppies, pursued
by no worshippers
but no blasphemers either
no one to sully

its void, a last-chance
god who will gather us
into the darkness
yet demand nothing of us
and bless us with
sweet fuck all?

Return of the First Person

At 50, hoping to make room
for something huge
I barred myself
from my poems

until whatever I
was preparing for
became bigger
than humility
larger than love
and more
than mere absence

Whole pages
were consumed by it
from the centre out

Nothing I threw into it
could fill that hole: stone
mountain, ocean or star
The void grew larger
than anything I understood

It needs me here
if only for what
I do not know

The Task

Each dawn
begins the search
for a word
by which he might
soothe himself
back into sleep

Day after day,
he boldly fills his lungs

Come dusk, he crawls
within reach of the dark
and exhales
silence
shaped like a man

If Memory Serves

When there was no chance of thunder   no chance
of that dark green sky   when there was
the silver grey   the blue dry   a tan chalk   the no chance
the dealer's day   the earth's   and not the sky's
chance of thunder   ice and thunder   illuminated ice
and sky no chance   but just a day and that
and silver   blue   and tan and dry
the dealer's call   no chance

Ars Brevis

blue paint blue
stone blue flame
from the torch

In truth: flailing
my arms, carving
air —

the words, once
again, too
small

Because

for Robert Lax

now
I must be
an old poet

a character
of bones
and hair

fingers shaped
by pens
and pencils

An old poet
all angles
with no

angle, I'll
watch the boats
the dogs

and summon
some
names

know
what I
know

Notes

The Ash Lad: In Norwegian legends, the ash lad is the resented youngest son for whom there is no inheritance, everything having gone to his older brothers. He strikes off on his own to seek his fortune. He succeeds magnificently after performing some heroic deed.

Stranded: Refers in part to the lovely theory that the evolution of flowering plants made it possible for early life to leave its aquatic environment and survive on land.

Cendrars' Hand: French writer Blaise Cendrars (1887-1961) lost an arm in the First World War, and in a poem called "Travel Notes," conflated the constellation Orion with his lost hand.

For the Record: Poet Paul Celan (1920-1970) was born Paul Antschel in what is now Romania. He briefly went by Paul Ancel and then, following the Second World War, took on the name by which he is known.

The Death of Saint-Denys Garneau: Hector de Saint-Denys Garneau (1912-1943) was a French-Canadian poet, devastated by the publication of his own first book — he felt he had somehow betrayed himself. He died of a heart attack beside a river not far from a cabin he was building.

After Guillevic: Eugène Guillevic (1907-1997) was a Breton poet.

The Ring of Brodgar: The Ring of Brodgar is an approximately 5,000-year-old circle of standing stones in the Orkney Islands of Scotland. Jodrell Bank in Cheshire, England, and Arecibo in Puerto Rico are the sites of major radio-astronomy observatories.

Relevance: Peter Huchel (1903-1981) was a German poet who was drafted into Hitler's army during the Second World War, incarcerated in a Russian POW camp, then persecuted by the Communist government of East Germany in the 1960s. He emigrated to West Germany in 1971.

Because: Robert Lax (1915-2000) was an American minimalist poet who lived for many years on the Greek islands of Patmos and Kalymnos and was revered for his calm Christian spirituality.

Acknowledgements

Some of the poems in this book appeared in *The Exile House*, published by Salmon Publishing Ltd., Cliffs of Moher, Co. Clare, Ireland, 2001 (http://salmonpoetry.com). They are reproduced here with the kind permission of the publisher.

Some of these poems also appeared in *The Laws of Gravity* (Reference West/Hawthorne Society), and in *Cendrars' Hand* and *The Ash Lad* (both of Alpha Beat Press). Others have appeared in the anthologies *Writing North* (Beluga Books), *Insights: Cultures* (Harcourt Brace Canada Ltd.), *Up from the Permafrost* (Yukon Learn), and *The Lost Whole Moose Catalogue #1* and *Urban Coyote: A Yukon Anthology* (both of Lost Moose Publishing). Some of the new poems have appeared in *Books in Canada*, *Out of Service*, *ICE-FLOE: International Poetry of the Far North* (USA), and *Shearsman* (UK). I would like to thank all these publishers and editors for their support.

My thanks to Lotteries Yukon and the Yukon Arts Branch for Advanced Artist Awards, which encouraged and sustained me.

The Writer-in-Residence program of Yukon Public Libraries brought Patricia Robertson and Brian Brett north and into my life, for which I'll always be grateful.